The Book of Props

Also by Wayne Miller

Only the Senses Sleep

The Book of Props

poems

Wayne Miller

milkweed
editions

Published 2009 by Milkweed Editions
Printed in Canada
Cover design by Travis Stearns
Author photo by Jeanne Ouellette
Interior design by Connie Kuhnz,
BookMobile Design and Publishing Services
The text of this book is set in Electra.
09 10 11 12 13   5 4 3 2 1
First Edition

Please turn to the back of this book for a list of the sustaining funders of Milkweed Editions.

Library of Congress Cataloging-in-Publication Data

Miller, Wayne, 1976–
        The book of props : poems / Wayne Miller.—1st ed.
            p.   cm.
        Includes bibliographical references and index.
        ISBN 978-1-57131-435-2 (pbk.: alk. paper)
        I. Title.
        PS3613.I56245B66 2009
        811'.6—dc22
                                        2008023327

This book, too, is for Jeanne—

and for my grandmother, Florence Arcuri.

There was an insolid billowing of the solid.
Night's moonlight lake was neither water nor air.
—Wallace Stevens

And what nonexistence holds is higher than our own
Existence, and it reaches us like ice and music.
—Tomas Venclova

The Book of Props

I.

II.

III.

IV.

(Three Codas)

Acknowledgments

Thanks to the editors of the following publications, where these poems previously appeared, sometimes in earlier versions:

Barrow Street: "Still Lifes and ____scapes"; *Born Magazine:* "Notes on the Night Highway (II)" (in conjunction with digital work by artist Dave Richardson and music by Justin R. Durban); *Boulevard:* "Notes on the Night Highway (I)"; *Crazyhorse:* "The Book of Props," "Dear Villon," "Lawn Chair Meditation (V)"; *Epoch:* "The Angels," "Pine Street"; *FIELD:* "Nocturne"; *Hotel Amerika: "from* 'Sleep Suite' (Prelude, History, Love, Coda)"; *Interim:* "Nude Asleep in the Tub"; *The Journal:* "Clarence and Da Vinci"; *Kulture Vulture: "from* 'Sleep Suite' (Language, Culture, Love, Death)"; *The Laurel Review:* "The Dream Maker," "The Tightrope Walker [walking across America]"; *Literary Imagination:* "Machado *Glosa*"; *The Melic Review:* "Andy, Alone in the City," "Clarence Playing"; *Meridian:* "Street Festival"; *New Orleans Review:* "In the Poem He No Longer Lives In,"; *Poetry:* "Walking through the House with a Candle,"; *Sycamore Review:* "Pinning Down the Notes"; *Whiskey Island Magazine:* "Dismantling the Scarecrow."

What Night Says to the Empty Boat (Notes for a Film in Verse) was published (in a previous version) as a chapbook by GreenTower Press. Thanks to the editors for their beautiful work; special thanks to John Gallaher.

"The Book of Props" received the Lucille Medwick Memorial Award from the Poetry Society of America. Thanks to Maury Medwick, Vijay Seshadri, and the PSA.

"Clarence Playing" partially inspired, and was incorporated into, "Map of Rain Hitting Water," a piece by composer Mara Gibson.

Some of this book was written with the support of a Ruth Lilly Fellowship from the Poetry Foundation and a C. Glenn Cambor Fellowship from Inprint, Inc.; my gratitude to both organizations and to Ms. Ruth Lilly.

Thanks to Daniel Slager for believing in this book, to James Cihlar for his careful and generous edits and suggestions, and to all the other folks at Milkweed for their outstanding work and dedication. Thanks, too, to Marianne Swierenga, my wonderful editor at New Issues whom I somehow forgot to thank in the acknowledgments to *Only the Senses Sleep.*

Finally, for their invaluable insights, support, and encouragement, thanks to Kevin Prufer, Brian Barker, Eric Williamson, Murray Farish, Whitney Terrell, Randall Mann, Hadara Bar-Nadav, Debra Di Blasi, Michelle Boisseau, Matthew Eck, Phyllis Moore, Jiří Cêch, Greg Oaks, Pablo Peschiera, Sean Hill, Marc McKee, Peter Covino, Kathleen Jesme, Rick Barot, Melichar, Brett Reif, Mara Gibson, Mom and Dad, and, of course, Jeanne.

The Book of Props

I.

Sleep Suite
[Prelude]

Light pressed to the tangle of birds
and branches and parked cars,

shop mannequins pinned
to the street (the street floating
like oil there in the glass—);

light striking the faces
of dogs and passersby, the leaves,
the radiator, the whitewashed sill;

light ringing them into existence
as a bell struck in a quiet room
rings one's hearing into existence;

light that keeps falling to ring
and ring the world
into world,—and all the while

a breeze passing through the light
untouched by it, asleep—

[*History*]

And somewhere in that tangle,
      a girl in a red hat sang along

to her earphones as it snowed
      from the sky's lit ceiling.

Passing her, I recognized
      the song, and when our paths

glanced and parted, I thought
      (in my loneliness) that perhaps

we were linked by the words
      I now sang in my head.

I held us in this thought
      until I forgot the next verse,

and then, all around me,
      the buildings were sleeping

by standing—

[Language]

So take for instance these words

twisted through the limbs of letters—

even on this open page

by the time you're finished

how many of them are sleeping?

[*Culture*]

When the man was beaten to death
                        on the quay below my room

I was fast asleep. I imagine
                        his shouts as flashbulbs

striking the river. Perhaps fifty feet from me,

and still my senses refused to open. The language

in which I'd learned to order
                        local meals and cocktails

was just the roomlight I'd slept in, quietly
                        dreaming—

[*Love*]

On their first date, they sat outside
at a café; as they sat there

they continued to move. Soon,
candlelight domed around them,

waiters appeared and disappeared
in a distant world above them;

they tasted their entrées, clicked
their eyelids in unwilled agreement.

Then we in the humanscape
blurred away. We can assume

that after dinner they stumbled
upon a first kiss. And later,

when the evening was over
and the city slept at last, nothing

had changed for us, and they
would never be the same.

[*Love*]

Cars swung past the open window
as the world ticked
                    in the rain

and the clock, and I suspect
in the neighbor's
                    pacemaker. Also:

your breathing, and the carlights
sliding the window's
                    projection around

on the wall. The corner vendor
arranged his oranges
                    in the predawn

quiet; then even
your sleeping face
                    was in motion —

like the fan
spinning its still,
                    translucent circle.

[*Death*]

Out where the wheat fields met the road,
a wood door lay flat on its back: pink
paint faded and peeling, brass knob

blackened and lying off by the shoulder.
You mentioned its beauty, which was
undeniable, and we imagined the house

in which it once had served as a valve
between—what rooms? what eyes?
You took comfort in thinking

of the hands that had touched it—
lovers' hands, children's hands—
but all I could see was the hard light

smacking it to an unbearable
brightness—the same light that once
struck it through a window.

[*Coda*]

I opened the drawer of the room

by turning out the lights. Earlier,
there'd been a train, a tented field,

and lots of drinks at a wedding.
All of which deflated like the light-

filled tent: a parachute whose cargo
had landed. A streetlamp

pressed the shadow of a tree
to the window screen, the same shadow

also on the bedside wall.
They rocked with the wind in tandem,

myself wedged between them
in that spare room I returned to

and then returned in the morning.

Dear Villon,

Though the rooms change,
we carry the old thoughts into them:

the snow of this morning
spills clear through the gutters,

draining the landscape
of white. Today, the dead breathe

their faces through chemical paper,
which is where they live

when their tattoos have left them.
(I hope you understand,

you who lay down
in your snowprint, only to have it

melt from around you.) Here,
many believe they'll die painlessly—

even as they roll on their lathes.
While our arguments save us

from *nothing*—(which explains
why you gave your mother

the best case for her soul you had).
I know: each shadow is lost

without the ground it lands on,
but leaves are blowing

where the snow just was,
and newspapers keep sealing

the expressions of the dying.
Tonight, I'll drink to your silent

arrival into my tomorrow.
Which will save a small piece

of the world for us — just us.
Though now this, too,

is in the language of thieves.

Notes on the Night Highway (I)

I passed Mail Pouch barns, scarred-
over fields, ponds of front yards
and the steps rising from them,—all drawn
from the darkness by houselights.

———

Windows: backlit wax—dimmest
of awakenings—as trucks hovered
in the rearview like phantoms
of Chinese dragons. Each moment

———

was scientifically pinpointed
by odometer and milemarker,
though I found myself guided more clearly
by the pale thrust of my headlights.

———

In an empty Clark station, raindrops
on the windshield found each other
and coalesced like a town's light,
like the words of a conversation on the radio.

———

Across the street was the only theater,
where a blank screen waited
for the marbled kiss that would infuse it
with motion. And this

———

was our civilization—the sky's reflection—
each lit town mirroring a star. As if
caught in the dream of a child, I followed
the breadcrumb reflectors,

———

I sliced along the dotted line
as the directions indicated. . . .

Walking Through the House
with a Candle,

I'm wading in the pupil of my life.

The rooms slide around compasslike,
shadows magnetically repelled

from my lit hand. Each blank wall
reveals the candle's lip—a dark

ledge on which the room rests.
Outside, the flash-veins of lightning

like sudden facts have all but passed.
What's left is a steady rain

of sound—malleable: hollowed
against the deck, fingertipped on brick,

indiscernible in the mowed grass.
My anticipation of life resuming—

the snap-to of the radio, the lights
sterilizing the rooms of all inversions—

stashes time on the blacked-out shelves.
In the lull, the house has changed:

the nailholes in the living room
have deepened into navels,

the floor's scattered papers
have swallowed their ordered print.

The bay window reflects my light
back into this shifting space,

of which I am for the moment
so indisputably the center.

Nocturne

Tonight all the leaves are paper spoons
in a broth of wind. Last week
they made a darker sky below the sky.

The houses have swallowed their colors,
and each car moves in the blind sack
of its sound like the slipping of water.

Flowing means falling very slowly—
the river passing under the tracks,
the tracks then buried beneath the road.

When a knocking came in the night,
I rose violently toward my reflection
hovering beneath this world. And then

the fluorescent kitchen in the window
like a page I was reading—a face
coming into focus behind it:

my neighbor locked out of his own party,
looking for a phone. I gave him
a beer and the lit pad of numbers

through which he disappeared; I found
I was alone with the voices that bloomed
as he opened the door. It's time

to slip my body beneath the covers,
let it fall down the increments of shale,
let the wind consume every spoon.

My voice unhinging itself from light,
my voice landing in its cradle—.
How terrifying a payphone is

hanging at the end of its cord.
Which is not to be confused with sleep—
sleep gives the body back its mouth.

II.

Notes on the Night Highway (II)

The sky can't hold the electricity forever—

it keeps spilling out. In Oklahoma,
the radio tower lost beneath its flashing

light was a dark web I knew to be there
(though the lit house on the black hill

never quite landed in its thought—).
Trucks sleeping by the highway wonderfully

express the drivers sealed inside them—
when we drifted by, I put this into words

as passing headlights filled your hair.
I try to believe we live in love's body—

so when it forgets us, we're still organs
pulsing for its life. My father claims

the past is in us, while my mother
claims it holds us. In the right hands,

a row of shrubs can turn into animals
and then the wind will stroke their fur.

A sculptor's chisel pierces stone exactly
to its sculpture. I must remember

that by holding you, I prepare to let you go—
even when lightning lifts the fields

sharply into view, I must remember
how we slide through them—

Pine Street

Then I arrived far from the ocean,

where the backdrop noise was empty.
No longer could I watch the lighthouse

dim itself by reeling in the morning,
nor would the sky lie down before me

all the way out to its own thin origin.
Slowly things surfaced into themselves—

the woodpile in the back alley
growing and diminishing, the neighbor's

wheat field rising above the blades
that would cut it down. I made my place

like a spider crossing the kitchen table—
a few needles of contact, the rest

just shadow. And when the first snow
dusted down, the frosted soil caught it,

and when I kissed again, my whole
being rose up to fill my mouth. Though

the trees rose and fell with their leaves,
the city kept shimmering behind them.

How far away I was. I carried my heart
like an ocean in a purse, unable

to hold it still. At night, crystals of ice
gathered on the surface of the lake,

the same dark surface stars were crossing.
For a time it seemed as if the stars

had doubled there — (though later,
while I was asleep, the ice erased them).

Nude Asleep in the Tub

As if she were something *opened*—
like a pocket watch—her body

slipped beneath a surface
peeled back to reveal its surface—

drops of air clinging to her thighs
like roe. Outside, the snow

pressed down against the city's
rooftops; a frozen shirt

on the clothesline hung slack,
no longer cracked and whipped

by the wind. And the window
just a slide of silence—its slip

into evening measured
in drips from the tap. I found

I was alone with her body—
refracted and clarified—water

breathing with her breath.
What could I do but watch

the lightwebs lambently drift
along the walls?—as if

the room's edges radiated
from her, as if I were inside

her thought. But then,
even before this could register,

the clothesline creaked
and the wind picked up,

and she stirred, so the water
broke from her into water.

Pinning Down the Notes

Beyond the levee, the water swallows itself,

swallows the reflections of stars.

Sound thins to a thread,
                              then past it

to breaking; to clothes

stitched onto a body

of chords, which disappears—suddenly

bodiless garment.
                      So allow

for the car's dark hood—for the dim light

it buries when the passing wind holds us.

Your knee on my knee, my hand

on the glass, your face

in the instant like light on a river.

The room will be the ghost of right now

for as long as we carry it. Yes,

this drift above the upright's footprints

and the instruments

in the hard light like our bodies
                                    invisibly

full of feeling for a while —

The Book of Props

Then the hammer explained
the arm's strange gestures,

and the hanging frames
hinted at walls that served

as frames. The glasses
left out on the brownstone

stoop caught light
as we passed by, and so

we gave them great
significance. Later,

in the unfamiliar dark
of a stranger's house,

I found the stairwell
by running my fingers

along the edge of a table.
Out back, people

were smoking, drinking
from painted bottles

as they pumped wood
into the chimenea.

O the songs they sang—
as still the fountain

poured water-sounds
out into the dark street

and the bay lured travelers
to pause on its midnight

ferry. All the saints
kept wringing themselves

through the contortions
of their names. Even

as the undertaker
undressed his childhood

sweetheart in preparation,
even as the trenches

grew into monuments,
then the monuments

into disrepair,—we knew
about the body

and the soul that fills it
with its own idea.

But what of the bed of nails,
the net of red marks

the audience admires?
What of the old man

lying there, counting
sheep in comradeship

with the shepherd? Now
the cup is held aloft,

and now the blood
comes pouring? Please—

come along to the garden,
we'll sniff the flowers,

let the birds chirp us
into romance. I'll put

a dandelion in your hair.
And when the cars

slip past like sharks,
we'll mock their glowing

ground effects; and when
the pistol is waved

in the air, we'll watch
the shimmering

of the runners' shoes.
How we longed to be

those lovers in the cab's
back seat, unmindful

of the driver thumbing
his matchbook—.

—Those poor lovers
drifting sexward in a river

of lights: now even
their kiss has become

another object pressed
between them.

Still Lifes and _____scapes

1.

Windows across the parkway.

                    How a body mars the perfect

rectangle of a door.
Or the sound of a passing car

cutting a line through the neighbors'
stereo. Then the notes,

the maple seeds—. Tonight,

2.

even the sound of the wind chimes
is geometric — each tone

the same shape
in a different register — ringing

shadows against the wall. Now
the gray fuzz of rain

falling beneath the streetlight
forms an image

of the sound of rain
hitting the street. And the water

beading on the chimes,
which are cold to the touch

and slicked with glow. I love
how this means

they've changed since yesterday;
I love how this does nothing

to alter their sound. Now

3.

clouds tarp their way across
the city's billow of light. The bridges

draw their shadows onto the river,
then the hills etched

with smokestacks and road lines.
How the wind whips

along the seams of traffic,
windows hanging

from the ribs of buildings.
See our reflections

there before the mannequins—
how we slide along

in our melisma.
Where's the *here* of history?—

4.

here, where the crane hoists its lights
above the museum,

and the wind knocks
the bottles off the porch

while we sleep? Here,
where the sun ices

the photographs on the shelf,
or the sound of rain

on the guttered leaves? Here,
where the snowscape

I imagine lives in the window
I open when I close

the sensory room? Here,
where a moment reveals

just a skin of patina—
no bronze beneath, no cold

and no core, though it holds
its shape—so delicate,

5.

so delicate? When
the snowscape comes, the park

will spill like a river
of whitewash. The cars will slip

alongside in their channels—
just beginning at the edges

to slush. Footprints will bloom
on the sidewalks

and stoops, crystals
blistering the white surface.

In the afternoon, when the trees
are at their starkest,

we'll ruin the field
by wading out into it,

6.

while elsewhere in the city,
a painter will be painting a still life.

She'll have gathered some fruit,
glass cups, scallop shells,

a blue china dish—.
As her construction begins

to reflect in the canvas,
she'll have to choose one

instant's shadowfall; from there,
the day will begin to sift

away from the painting.
Then, later, when she's satisfied

her work is a window
onto her things, without a thought,

she'll destroy the room's echo
of the canvas by taking

a bite of the apple. Of course,
I mean this

7.

as an echo of myth. Let's say a man
stands before Rembrandt's *Danaë*,

which he's loved all his life
from looking at textbooks. Now

that it's right here before him,
he doesn't see much

more than he did on the page.
He's viewing its present—

and he can't understand
why this, the original,

is more important to see—
though he fears losing it

the moment he turns away.
From the window,

8.

the lit windows across the park
don't form a pattern—

I know,
I've been looking. Dear lover,

your face in its present expression
means what I think

the expression means—
but maybe I'm wrong. The city

watches us into this existence,
and I can picture you

laughing, though I can't
now remember at what. Sometimes

words are more fleeting
than the images behind them,

and the passing bass of a car
can almost hold the night

inside it. All those lights.
When one goes out,

it leaves a black window,

9.

which opens onto a room—
where everything lies

as the sleeper(s) left it.
Where the table is a plinth

holding objects up to the carlights
that slide across them

in glances, without warning,
where empty chairs

crowd the table (perhaps one lies
overturned), where

curtains billow above the vent,
or the radiators crack

arhythmically, where a dishwasher
slips through its cycles.

The alarm clock is set—

III.

What Night Says to the Empty Boat

(Notes for a Film in Verse)

[*We lay there without moving. But under us all moved, and moved us, gently, up and down, and from side to side.*
—Samuel Beckett]

In Traffic on the Kansas Turnpike

1.

Shot from inside the car: a monarch
paused on the windshield, and a scarecrow

in a roadside field (narrow aperture
so they're both in focus). Andy driving

and mouthing along to a song—line
of brake lights sparking—as Justine
turns toward Clarence in the back. Fade.

2.

Shot of the road, now from above, cars
inching like segments of a dragged chain.

Two angels visible at the screen's edge,
perched up high on the cornstalk tips.

A cloud slides in to stain the scene
a dark blue; as the camera pulls back,
a thresher is swallowed into view. Fade.

3.

Shot from just outside the car: Justine
leaning back toward Clarence as he lights
her cigarette with a match. A cloud

of smoke through the clouds on the glass,
and when she says, *Thanks* (which we

can't hear), the breath behind
the word blows out the flame. Fade.

The Tightrope Walker

                              walking across America
on telephone wires will be an important
symbol. Each night, on the living-room TV,

a quick shot of him stepping over
Scranton, Youngstown, Toledo, Joliet
(and a bit of the accompanying commentary).

Near the end, Justine will look out
the window and there he'll be—approaching
her roof—his balancing pole held out

before him like a broken mast. She'll phone
Clarence then—her words streaming
beneath the walker's feet. She'll say

something like: *Who'll know if he falls*
in Nebraska, or Wyoming—after the news
forgets him? Clarence's reply: *Perhaps two lovers*

—like us—talking across the country, will hear
a trembling in their voices,
as the quivering wire upsets the birds—

Justine's Childhood

She and her mother followed cement trucks—they called
them *turnips on wheels*, or *babies of Mrs. Hubbard's shoe.*
Justine was obsessed; her mother indulged her curiosity.

Late in August, they trailed one for more than two hours,
out to where the suburbs met the country. The truck slowed
near some workers laying a sidewalk along an empty field,

and then the cement came pouring. Justine was transfixed—
she'd never seen what was in those trucks, and she loved
how the workers smoothed the cement with their floats.

Mom stared blankly across the field (Wyeth-like,
with a few pecking birds and a barn way up on the hill),

while back home, Dad pulled into the empty driveway,
an old sprinkler sputtering in the yard. Then a shot

of the mixer rotating on its hollow axis, and the sun
channeling its light down the furrows in the field.

The Angels

The angels spend most of their time
on earth with their coworkers the scarecrows.

They have a lot to talk about, and of course
plenty of complaints:

most commonly, they're too light—so often
they're swept up by a passing wind.

(At least the scarecrows are posted down.)

And what are they made of?—all that
dust and straw and powdered lapis. All that

essence dries their throats. One finds
he's up all night longing for a glass of water.

A shot of Gabriel shaking his head
in the moonlight: *It's not what I expected,*

he says, still watching the house
across the field, where a window has filled

with the underwater light of a television.
The scarecrow shrugs on his cross—

Ain't what I expected either, he mutters
through his sewn mouth.

Justine's Childhood (Abroad)

[Two brief scenes]

1.

The hanging lights warp
in the curve of the pastry case;

behind it, the café's matron —
a thin puff of flour

risen from her apron. Here,
the language is like rain

outside a window, the drops
joined in one body,

a blank presence.
Only her mother's words

cut through: *maybe pastina*
with broth, an omelet?

2.

A tiny sloop that belongs
to her mother's dear friend —

Justine against the coaming,
up from the tiller, watching

the sail's shadow slip over
the water. The rippling chop

enhances the shadow's
illusion of fluttering. Though,

It's only the sail that flutters,
Justine says to herself—

the shadow's untouched
by the wind that propels it.

Andy, the Drawbridge Operator

His WPA bridge lifts vertically

from the two puzzle pieces of shore. Iron counterweights

descend as it rises, his cockpit hung in girders

above the roadway. What he likes is the visceral—

the barges shouldering the narrow river, the rust

like magnetized ash, the steel rivets

of another age bulleted through the frame.

And there's something to be said for the isolation—

car engines dull and distant, strangers

sliding past on their threads. But for Andy,

the work has lost its thrill—pulling a lever

now seems too easy a way to withdraw

the bridge's illusion of permanence.

Andy's Monologue

Talking to another man at a bar
is like talking to the driver on an all-night
road trip—eye contact's impossible,
you're both so focused on the dim light
filling the bottles before the mirror.

What's said isn't all that important,
so long as you're both here, and staying
awake. And we're doing that now,
you and me, thinking about what things
we've lost—and of course talking

about whatever else happens to mind.
Notice that line in the beer swirling—
Guinness over Bass, Irish over English
—as if that matters to us here
in this thin Midwest darkness,

night clinging like ergot to the chaff.
Look at those sportscasters there:
job's giving name to "virtue—I mean
the Renaissance kind—each player
holding action like a sort of potion

in the flask of his body. What we've done
becomes us—I know this—: exercise
becomes muscles, and, bless it,
touching a woman sometimes becomes
feelings. [He points to an instant

replay above him on the screen.]
See how he holds onto it?—that's
perfection. And I say thank God for it—
for those men who stay in motion above us
each Sunday, while we get good

and drunk.

Justine's Window

At night from the outside—Justine there doing a crossword—

alternated with shots of animated letters rising like fish to surface

in the puzzle's little windows—(as if nibbling the pen's felt tip).

Raindrops slash the glass between us and her, soon giving way

to blur. And then we can barely hear the music she's listening to,

drowned as it is by the raindrops losing themselves

in the tin clamor of rain against the air conditioner—

The Dream Maker

We'll see her hand paused

indecisively over an endless table

on which lies a mélange of silver

surgeon's tools, bits of nest matter,

cuttings of film negatives, cubes

of rusted iron, disembodied

buttons, a collapsed preschool-

quality mobile, empty test tubes,

underlit slides, feathers floating

in pools of mercury—and whatever

else we can gather to give

the impression of tactile surreality,

all set out like the parts of some

great and disassembled machine.

Clarence's Soliloquy

We caught twelve bluegills the day my father
took me out to a friend's pond,
where he tried to cultivate in me his love of fishing.
I think he was afraid one day we'd stop talking.

He carried the fish up to the barn, where in the dim,
dry light, he taught me to scrape off the scales,
cut down behind the gills, feel each bone
against the blade as you slice toward the tail.

I'd wanted to throw them back—we both knew
they were too small to eat. "No, it's good practice,"
he said, and I went on, his eyes following
my hands,—the white flesh left there in the hay.

Prospect Street

                     —snow falling,
tire tracks leaving the driveway,
footprints to the empty space
where the car has been.

A tin pan of motor oil
lies next to the latticed porch, —
oil the color of winter trees.

Snow continues to fall, slowly
the tire tracks leave the driveway.

Aerial View of the City

The ground, a yellow and tan
                    woven into being by its arrival

into the oval window; then the city
                    like an open hand

(Justine points out), the plane's shadow
            just a finger tracing the surface.

It's like a painting of a city,
            Andy will say, *as if we're at the end*

of a hallway making out a picture. And indeed, the city

will be still—like her childhood
            memories of that city—as the camera

passes over and they descend—
           no real movement down there at all—

even as the plane slips by, sliding
                the city past—

until they land and give it their motion—

Street Festival

Where the tips of the palm fronds are frayed into hair—

Where the sparklers will rise into ash from the dark—

Where the windows are blisters of dusk on the street—

Where the sound of the river gives sound to the light—

Where Justine is a sliver of flesh through her mask—

Where the music is flesh, where the music is flesh

that gives blood to desire— Where desire is a mask

they will wear in their thoughts— Where the crowd

gives voice to the air in their breath— Where Andy

will press his glass to her neck— Where the crowd

slides around them in fingers of sound— Where

the crowd is a surface that holds up the night—

Where the cars are like ghosts that wander the streets—

Where the cab is a ghost that will carry them on—

Clarence at Work

He's turned the hallway closet into an office

with a desk (the classroom kind), a snapshot
from Kelleys Island, and the photo
of Justine he took behind the East Pine.

The clock radio plays some recognizable
tune through interstation fog,

while he empties his bucket into the deep
sink, a length of orange hose
attached to the faucet. Now a shot

of him walking away, framed by the gray
museum hallway he's gone over

four nights a week for the last
eleven years. So he can see his face in it.

Traveling Shot through
the Snowfields at Dusk

A dark fence, and for a moment the scarecrow

with snow peaked on his shoulders. Then,

Clarence in his car, the fields growing steadily

darker. Soon there's just the narrow funnel

of light the car pushes before it—until

a snow truck appears. Zoom in on the sparks

skittering off the blade of the plow,

landing against the snowbank. We'll hold

on these flakes of light (high shutter speed

so there's no motion blur) as they erase

all the snowflakes they touch—then,

inevitably, are put out by them.

Justine and the Lava Rocks

Her silhouette growing out of the rocks
like a scarecrow
in a field of wheat.

Andy farther below, barefoot,
holding a camera.
What are you doing,

Justine? he asks as he watches her
lift a piece
of rock in her hand. Pan

left, to take in more light, wash
out the screen,
the waves splashing

the rocks behind her. *This liquid*
breathed down
into the sea, she says,

and so it lost its breath. . . .

Clarence and Da Vinci

Da Vinci believed the stars
could be studied in the surface
of a still lake—their distances
collapsed like speech

to a page, their needlelights
candles in the fingers
of the drowned. From the shore,
a piece of the sky is there,

but once Clarence rows out,
the lake holds every star
facing this side of the earth.
—Except those burying

themselves in the boat,
and he can't still himself
enough to stop the sky
from rocking—so clear now—

how wrong they must have been
who thought it steady.

Andy, Alone in the City

A church,
then an awning,
then a dog
licking a stain
from a cobblestone,
windows through
which strangers
obliquely mirror
the recognizable,
an empty fountain
full of dry leaves,
a corner—motorcycle
firing itself away—,
steps to a hospital
(or a school), a beautiful
girl descending
along an iron rail,
a sidewalk café—chairs
pressed to the wall
as if by the wind—,
a word he understands
from the mouth
of an old woman,
then her son, an ice-
cream cart, a sewer's
stink rising like water,
a hawker hawking
for a strip club, a hostel,
a day spa, a cigarette
tossed deliberately
from a balcony,

a yellow wall
catching the light—
taking his breath—,
a butcher sawing
through bone, a kid
with a busted lip
rushing past,
knocking Andy down,
so he must rise
and check his hands
for grit, one by one
gather up
his belongings—

What Night Says to the Empty Boat

[To be projected into the rowboat
        Clarence has left floating in the slip—]

I will press you to the water.

                I will press you to the water,

and when the water rises,

you will rise, and when the water falls—.

                I will be the water,

beneath the water that holds you.

Feel the wind in the waves

that lap at your prow? I will stay with you

all day. I will sleep in your shadows—

in the shadows of oars. You will keep me alive—

I will whisper their squeaking.

                And when I curl

in your hull, you will bow with my weight.

I will hook my stars

        in the water beneath you,

in the skim of water that floats here within you.

        And this is the way,

believe me, we will not disappear.

Landing

This city
like a nickel of light
dropped in a field.
Justine pictures

the drive back home,
and Clarence
doing what?—
perhaps, too, driving

the empty roads
from work, perhaps
rising to meet her
as she steps through

his door. What
words will arrive
before them,
like the city growing

up from the dark,
approaching—.
How little this plane
means to that body

of light. How essential
that light is
to all of them
there on the plane.

Dismantling the Scarecrow

At first: the mouth still sewn,
the voice inside with the straw
the farmer pulls and scatters

across the barn floor, the sackface
a few weeks later burned
in the bonfire, the shirt and jeans

tossed into the workbench's
bottom drawer. Only the grayed
hat continues to hold

some trace of the snow
that skimmed its brim, the pollen
and light that dusted it. The hat

left lying in a corner of the loft,
behind the musty bales
and a half-constructed engine.

When the next family moves in
their youngest son will pick it up,
lift it to his face as if

its smell perhaps might yield
some hint of history.
What he uncovers there, inside

that mute presence, will not be
the past (he imagines the hat
worn by a living man), but rather

his own echo—
like the light filling the windows
of the house across the field.

The Tightrope Walker

And then he's gone. Justine keeps watching

the line for movement. *Are you there?* Clarence asks,

and Justine nods without speaking. *Hello?—*

I'm here, and now the camera pans to her face

reflected in the glass, the outside world

visible through it. *I can't see him*, she says,

scanning the trees and houses down her street,

the yards and roofs stretching westward

far beyond what she can see, though she imagines

how the windows in that direction must be changing

color, yard by yard, from sunrise to clear.

Clarence Playing

When at last Justine arrives, he's at the piano.
The hammers strike and rise

with his fingers, and the pedal's damp
shifting carries through the instrument

as waves echo through the frame of a ship.
Outside, each car marks a moment's

passing, and when a muffler rattles
Justine looks out the window, then back

to Clarence as he presses into clay
the shape of another chord. He's always

imagined music as a sort of climbing —
by the song's end, he's reached into a brief

rapture of completion (as a child reaches
into a cabinet of sweets). Though

now he thinks perhaps the music's
more like a map of rain hitting water —

he's moving closer to her without moving;
and how wonderful to be held from her

at last by nothing but the song's duration —

IV.

(Three Codas)

Machado *Glosa*

To keep the wind working
he sewed the dead leaves back again —
this threading voice to mouth

long after the words were spoken.
Which too keeps the wind in motion,
as do the papers

blown skyward from my hands.
See how the snow's pulled down
by the leaves' falling,

how the curtains are opened
and closed by applause? A song
coheres because silence

seals the notes, just as snow
explains our footsteps, then
directs them walking home.

Watch a string become a wick
and still within the wax
remain a string. One summer,

the park taught me to ride a bicycle;
another, love fell through me
for the first time. I must

remember that *I* made the blur
in the time-lapse photograph of me,
just as dandelions draw

my breath toward their dispersal.
Now a small tree full of monarchs
is pulled into thought

by its mere existence, and yet
each surgery stitches us
closed with pain. Try to separate

the seeing from what's seen,
as if a pool shot could exist
without the balls. What we call

breath is only air, and Collioure
is just a town with a lighthouse church,
though Machado's footsteps

ended there. Watch a boat's
wake turn slowly back into sky,
then the sky back into water—:

see how what's seen must separate
from the seeing, these footsteps
sewn back into leaves,

these leaves back into wind?

Lawn Chair Meditation (V)

Now that today's nearly over,
the yard's grown into its details,

just as the hibiscuses have opened
into tenors for the vehicle

of *radar dish*. I'll never quite get
how the cellophane bags

of water hanging from the eaves
keep the flies away, though

I love how the dusklight
blisters in them, how the water

mimics the air around it
in a thicker, more clarified way.

The singer's voice arriving
from a great distance—right

here in the radio—; the chords
beneath the lyrics now shift

into clouds and light marbling
a bay. And now the passing

traffic thins on the highway,
and now the palms have almost

plastically begun to stir.
So enter the hummingbird: ruby-

throated flit of air rowing
around on the blur of its wings.

Just as the coiled hose could be
a painting of the water's flow,

the impatiens grip their fists
of seeds, each fist just waiting

to burst into symbol, for what—
the human heart? And when

I blow a dandelion clock apart,
it leaves in its place the idea

of dandelion. It's the idea
I now keep lifting to my cheek

to feel a whisper there—
and which, at the same time,

I find myself also longing
to blow apart.

In the Poem He
No Longer Lives In,

1.

the streets hang like frozen gestures,
and the flowers snap

silently into bloom; construction
has stopped—half-built

houses give off the scent
of pine, as rain clouds

erase the shadows and swirl
out toward the sea; bodies

sit facelessly in the cafés, watching
cars balloon in the drops

on the glass, while past lovers sink
more deeply into their lines

—as deeply as can be imagined—
and then a sunset

slicking down the mirrored sky-
scrapers, or else the river

beneath cloud cover—an endlessly
passing barge; in a doorway

by the tracks, a girl
holds a knife—the same knife

he saw from his car, the same girl
unaged and unkempt

as the stalls in the market, the wharfs
on the canal that can never

collapse since he's recorded them
intact; the swatches

in the jukebox flip like words,
faces around the tables,

and the mailman—just the line
of his blue through the street—

suspended above trains
threading the tunnels, beneath planes

rising and falling endlessly,
unnoticeable as leaves;

2.

the warehouses he photographed
are as stark as the pictures

he keeps in the filing cabinet,
as the voices to which he once

raptly adhered; in the room
where he slept, the water has boiled

off his dreams—they lie like shirts
on the floor—; and there

in the kitchen, above the blur
of traffic, that spring-pale

leaf remains pressed
to the window, all day lit up

with sunlight, then at night,
lit by whoever

inhabits the room—

Notes/Sources

Opening epigraphs: Stevens: "Reality Is an Activity of the Most August Imagination"; Venclova: "[As in a cloud: a lock, a glass of water, a chair,]" (trans. Diana Senechal).

"What Night Says to the Empty Boat (Notes for a Film in Verse)": Beckett epigraph from *Krapp's Last Tape*.

"Clarence and Da Vinci": *The Notebooks of Leonardo Da Vinci* (trans. Edward MacCurdy).

"Machado *Glosa*": "Proverbs," by Antonio Machado (translated loosely by Don Paterson in his book *The Eyes*).

Wayne Miller is the author of *Only the Senses Sleep* (New Issues, 2006), which received the 2007 William Rockhill Nelson Award, translator of Moikom Zeqo's *I Don't Believe in Ghosts* (BOA, 2007), and coeditor of the anthology *New European Poets* (Graywolf, 2008). His poems have appeared in *Barrow Street, Boulevard, Crazyhorse, Epoch, FIELD, The Gettysburg Review, The Paris Re-*

view, Poetry, on *Poetry Daily,* and elsewhere. The recipient of the George Bogin Award, the Lyric Poetry Award, and the Lucille Medwick Award from the Poetry Society of America, as well as the Bess Hokin Prize and a Ruth Lilly Fellowship from the Poetry Foundation, he lives in Kansas City and teaches at the University of Central Missouri, where he edits *Pleiades: A Journal of New Writing.*

More Poetry Books from Milkweed Editions

To order books or for more information, contact Milkweed at
(800) 520-6455
or visit our Web site (www.milkweed.org).

Music for Landing Planes By
Éireann Lorsung

Hallelujah Blackout
Alex Lemon

Willow Room, Green Door
Deborah Keenan

Black Dog, Black Night:
Contemporary Vietnamese Poetry
Nguyen Do and Paul Hoover, editors

Reading Novalis in Montana
Melissa Kwasny

Milkweed Editions

Founded in 1979, Milkweed Editions is one of the largest independent, nonprofit literary publishers in the United States. Milkweed publishes with the intention of making a humane impact on society, in the belief that good writing can transform the human heart and spirit.

Join Us

Milkweed depends on the generosity of foundations and individuals like you, in addition to the sales of its books. In an increasingly consolidated and bottom-line-driven publishing world, your support allows us to select and publish books on the basis of their literary quality and the depth of their message. Please visit our Web site (www.milkweed.org) or contact us at (800) 520-6455 to learn more about our donor program.

Milkweed Editions, a nonprofit publisher, gratefully acknowledges sustaining support from Anonymous; Emilie and Henry Buchwald; the Patrick and Aimee Butler Family Foundation; the Dougherty Family Foundation; the Ecolab Foundation; the General Mills Foundation; the Claire Giannini Fund; John and Joanne Gordon; William and Jeanne Grandy; the Jerome Foundation; the Lerner Foundation; the McKnight Foundation; Mid-Continent Engineering; a grant from the Minnesota State Arts Board, through an appropriation by the Minnesota State Legislature, a grant from the National Endowment for the Arts, and private funders; Kelly Morrison and John Willoughby; an award from the National Endowment for the Arts, which believes that a great nation deserves great art; the Navarre Corporation; Ellen and Sheldon Sturgis; Target; the James R. Thorpe Foundation; the Travelers Foundation; Moira and John Turner; U. S. Trust Company; Joanne and Phil Von Blon; Kathleen and Bill Wanner; Serene and Christopher Warren; and the W. M. Foundation.

Interior design by Connie Kuhnz,
Bookmobile Design and Publishing Services
Typeset in Electra by American type designer
William Addison Dwiggins
Printed on acid-free Rolland Enviro
(100 percent postconsumer waste) paper
by Friesens Corporation